Hi matt,
When you're feelin [...]
a funny cartoon and laugh.
Our Love & Prayers Are With You!
Dolores & Duane

LUNKERS!

John Troy

THE LYONS PRESS

Printed in the United States of America

10 9 8 7 6 5 4 3 2 1

The Library of Congress Cataloging-in-Publication Data is available on file.

"I like to think there's a lunker in each pool I fish."

"I can tell you, it wasn't easy."

"It's just amazing how something with a brain the size of a pea can easily outwit . . . shh, here comes another one."

"No, no, you dummy, you're supposed to hit *this* fly, not the ones on the hat!"

"If anybody catches that lunker, it'll probably be Herb."

"Couldn't you just show them the pictures?"

"I'd feel a lot better about catching that 40-pound muskie if it
hadn't eaten my 14-pound bass."

"You don't see many salmon runs like this one."

"So what's this I hear about you not shaving until you catch a muskie?"

"Oh, good, that saves us the trouble of coming to your house to see your muskie."

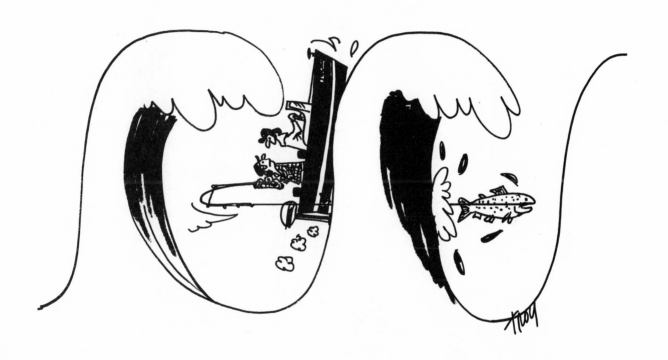

"I can't tell if it's jumping or sounding, but it's a salmon alright!"

"I caught a muskie before Herb did, since then life has been pure hell."

"Have you ever thought of just using a nice sucker for muskie bait?"

"I don't really care that you tie flies better than me, or that you can cast farther, or even that you catch more fish than I do. What gets me is that you look so damn good doing it."

Well, I've *hooked* a few muskies."

"To tell you the truth, we haven't even seen a *walleye*."

"Guess what I caught while I was trolling under the bridge?"

"It started out as a friendly talk on all fishermen being kindred spirits, then the trout fishermen suggested bass were trout with the brains taken out, so the bass fisherman wanted to know where the zipper was on a fly rod..."

"No, no, you idiot, it's plastic!"

"Forget the plastic worms."

"I just said we'd get there first, I didn't say we'd be able to stop."

"We got two small bass and three large speeding tickets."

"Hang in there, I think he's tiring."

"There you go again, horsing them in!"

"Trolling's out of the question, I can't do less than fifty-four miles an hour."

"Try by that old stump, there's usually a good one hiding there."

"I don't know which I like better, the marmalade or the grape."

"Anybody can get hooked in a tree, you can tell the real pros by how they get loose."

"This is my first year bass fishing."

"I think your line's too heavy."

"That reminds me, I'm supposed to go fishing for Largemouths with Ed."

"I'll be darn glad when bass season opens."

"By golly, you're right, the sonar *does* show 'structure' in the area."

"So rub it in, hotshot."

"Mixing a little business with pleasure this trip?"

"The fellow on the left favors the Smoke Red Metal Flake Auger Tail Jelly Worm, while the fellow on the right objects, feeling that the Electric Grape Squirm Worm Sidewinder is more productive."

"Did you whittle that plug from a broom handle, Jesse?"

"Edgar missed a bass-of-a-lifetime this morning, so talk about politics or religion."

"You didn't see a bass boat go by here about 60 miles per hour, did you?"

"George lives and breathes bass fishing."

"I'll be darned—there's my sinkers, my watch, my knife . . ."

"He's a lawyer, so don't even ask him how many fish he caught."

"Don't cast too close to shore or a damn frog will grab it."

"I see you like doing things the old-fashioned way."

"We can't get in—it'll sink."

"I don't like the looks of this fish, Bobby Joe."

"You're scaring the fish!"

"Fresh water, salt water, hell, fishin' is fishin'!"

"You want to troll, I want to fish the shoreline.
How do we solve this problem?"

"Trolling? I thought you said bowling."

"I think our cannonballs are bumping bottom!"

"Whoops, sorry fellas!"

"I get seasick."

"Ed's determined to high speed troll those lakers, no matter how deep they are."

"It was her late husband's most prized possession and she wouldn't part with it, so I bought the old lady, too."

"I run this on peanuts."

"Oh, lighten up, next time we'll *bring* a sonar."

"Who needs sonar?"

"Your rod's bone-jarring, hook-setting power impresses me no end. However ..."

"Did you say Off-the-road or Off-the-ground vehicle?"

"You can almost feel them biting, can't you?"

"I think you're a bit much on this camouflage thing."

"What's a guy like you doing with an earring?"

"Darn magnetic drag!"

"I forgot my fly rod."

"I used to have a boron rod, but the bank repossessed it."

"And here's a handy little item that goes nicely with your combination hunting and fishing license."

"Are you kidding? This new custom-made bamboo rod doesn't go *near* the river!"

"I spent half my life searching for the perfect rod. Finally I said the heck with it."

"George's belief is that all fish should be released to be caught another time. Some day he's going to catch one, to justify his philosophy."

"Bob likes to relive the moment."

"So what are you doing after the party?"

"We seldom eat fish. I don't like them, and George can't catch them."

"Will it help our relationship if I throw it back?"

"My only regret is that I had to give up fishing."

"Do I take this to mean, that your role as a 'fishing widow' has ended?"

"Home is the sailor, home from the sea . . ."

"Sure, but will you love me when fishing season is over?"

"Size 14, that must be a new record for this lake."

"Wouldn't you know it, just when they were biting good!"

"Hey, you idiot, you made me lose a nice fish!"

"If I don't get a hit soon I'm switching to an underwater lure."

"Suppose you do get it in the hole ... then what?"

"Okay, the first sonuvabitch that says 'How are they biting' is a dead man!"

"Wow, that was one helluva cast. Too bad your line wasn't attached to it."

"Wow, that's some backlash!"

"Every day I ask myself 'is it worth all that misery going out in the rottenest weather to catch a few lousy little fish?' . . . and before I can answer this idiot in me says 'Yup.'"

"You're not going to like this, pop, but I want to be a fly fisherman."

"These aren't the grubs, this is the noodle salad."

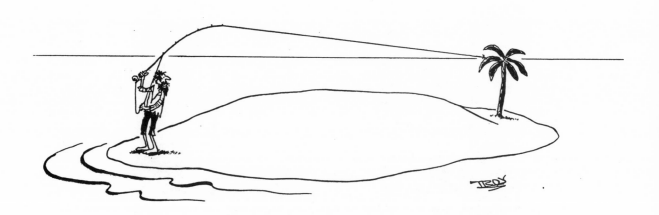

"Do you think that, somehow, they *know*?"

"I caught them on a size twelve Dark Hendrickson dry fly. What are you using?"

"He's strictly wet flies."

"Still determined to catch that lunker trout on a dry fly?"

"I was wasting away on booze and drugs—man, then I discovered fly fishing."

"Waiter, there's a fly in this soup."

"Say, I'm kind of new at this, how do you keep these flies on the hook?"

(Thanks to Wayne Nester for this memorable quote.)

"Pardon me, I couldn't help but notice your rod is falling below the one o'clock position during the backcast, your wrist is not straight, and you're dropping the rod tip too early on the forward cast which can result in not only wind knots, but also—say, you don't mind me telling you this, do you?"

"To give you an idea how bad it's been, *that* is a feeding frenzy."

"What are you using?"

"So who taught you how to tie flies?"

"Quick, hit the pocket over there with your Muddler!"

"For the love of God, man, switch to wets . . . they'll never rise in seas like this!"

"I'm from the IRS. I'll take one of those fish."

"So what *is* the limit, anyway?"

"I said, 'Let's see your license!'"

"A bait fisherman, eh—and just how did you slip through?"